Haiti Glass

Haiti Glass

Lenelle Moïse

City Lights Books | San Francisco

Cover art by Lenelle Moïse, untitled collage, 2013

Library of Congress Cataloging-in-Publication Data
Moïse, Lenelle, 1980-
  [Poems. Selections]
  Haiti glass / Lenelle Moise.
      pages cm. — (City lights/Sister spit)
    ISBN 978-0-87286-614-0 (pbk.)
    I. Title.

PS3613.O397A6 2014
811'.6—dc23

City Lights Books are published at the City Lights Bookstore,
261 Columbus Avenue, San Francisco, CA 94133.
www.citylights.com

contents

haiti glass

haiti glass
star in my mouth

beautiful burning
spiky light

wish so hard
scrapes my soft palate

tongue a shadow
of swollen loss

language of shards
flicker stutter

pronouncing the distance
rays bruise gums

mud mothers

the children of haiti
are not mythological
we are starving
or eating salty cakes
made of clay

because in 1804 we felled
our former slave captors
the graceless losers sunk
vindictive yellow
teeth into our forests

what was green is now
dust and everyone knows
trees unleash oxygen
(another humble word
for life)

they took off
with our torn branches
beheaded our future
stuck our breath up on pikes
for all the world to see

we are a living dead example
of what happens to warriors who
in lieu of fighting for white men's countries
dare to fight
for their own lives

during carnival
we could care less
about our bloated empty bellies
where there are voices
we are dancing

where there is vodou
we are horses
where there are drums
we are possessed
with joy and stubborn jamboree

but when the makeshift
trumpet player
runs out of rhythmic breath
the only sound left is
guts grumbling

and we sigh
to remember
that food
and freedom
are not free

is haiti really free
if our babies die starving?
if we cannot write our names
read our rights keep
our leaders in their seats?

can we be free? really?
if our mothers are mud? if dead

columbus keeps cursing us
and nothing changes
when we curse back

we are a proud resilient people
though we return to dust daily
salt gray clay with hot black tears
savor snot cakes
over suicide

we are hungry
creative people
sip bits of laughter
when we are thirsty
dance despite

this asthma
called debt
congesting
legendarily liberated
lungs

adaptation

What I remember about flying to New York from a Haiti I have not seen since I left, I do not actually remember, but craft from the photographs my father took and the words my mother claims are fact.

I wore a gown: crushed red velvet on top, layers of sheer white on the bottom. Panicked, Papi paid a pretty stranger in a fitted dress to sit beside me on a plane that flashed "American" on both sides.

Hours later, when we arrived, the bustle of J.F.K. Airport split me from my negligent escort. All alone, with newborn precision, I pushed through bodies on a foreign walkway, held my toddler-immigrant back as upright as arrogance, stepped as deliberate as martian feet and searched myriad expectant faces for a mother I barely knew.

I had only loved her through scented letters, sent from overseas and read aloud to me by my Papi—who could not join us, who could not fly, who had to adapt to losing love. Twice.

Mommi bellowed my nickname and I replied. Determined stride to frantic pounce. She held me tight. She wore blue silk and smelled of joy. Her kisses pressed my twitching cheek as a man I did not know said, "Welcome home," words I could not yet decipher.

He was her husband, a citizen. He had sponsored my legal exile, my buried flight, a right reunion. To repay him, I was required to call him, "Daddy."

So—gratefully, guiltily—I did.

the children of immigrants

When I am a toddler, a child, a tween, a teen, and a young adult, I am called an ancestral soul, a ti gran moun, a little old person.

Adults study me and decide that I am wise beyond my years, mature for my age, emotionally ripe. I am told it is unusual to meet a five-ten-fifteen-year-old girl who does not slouch or mumble or speak in monosyllables.

When I do the things that come naturally to me—when I hold my spine up erect, when I wait my turn to speak, when I speak having listened, carefully, when I enunciate, when I look grown-ups in the eye—I am told I must have "been here before."

"How do you know?" one college professor asks me after she has seen a psychologically violent play I have written at age nineteen. "How do you already know?"

In high school, I charm my teachers. They encourage me to write speeches about feminism that I recite for International Women's Day at City Hall or deliver as part of conference panels at local universities. "If you were older," they tell me, "we would probably be friends." One of them even flirts with me.

Among my peers I exist somewhere between amicably mysterious and irrevocably dorky. The popular kids greet me in the hallways, but they never invite me to their beer-drenched parties. I will never play Spin the Bottle. I will never play Seven Minutes in Heaven. My mother tells me she is protecting me from boys, but the truth is, after I do my homework, she wants me to type up another family friend's résumé or resignation letter. At home, I am a bridge, a cultural interpreter, a spokesperson, a trusted ally, an American who is Haitian too, but also definitely American.

The children of immigrants don't get to be children. We lose our innocence watching our parents' backs bend, break. I am an old soul because when I am young, I watch my parents' spirits get slaughtered.

In Haiti, they were middle class. Hopeful teachers. Home owners. They were black like their live-in servants. They donated clothes to the poor. They gave up everything they knew to inherit American dreams. And here, they join factory lines, wipe shit from mean old white men's behinds, scrub five-star hotel toilets for dimes above minimum wage. Here, they shuck and jive and step and fetch and play chauffeur to people who aren't as smart as they are, people who do not speak as many languages as they do. In the 1980s, they are barred from giving blood because newscasters and politicians say that AIDS comes from where they come from: Haiti, the poorest country in the Western Hemisphere, a black magic island that spawns boat people and chaos, a place of illiterate zombies, orphan beggars and brazen political corruption.

When I am a child, my childhood is a luxury my family cannot afford. Their dignity is not spared, so my innocence is not spared. They are humiliated and traumatized daily, so I become a nurse to their trauma. I am told too much, so I know too much, so I am wise beyond my years.

When I am six, my mother tells me that when she found out she was pregnant with me at age nineteen, she "tried to kill the baby." She says "the baby," as if it isn't me she's talking about; as if I am not the expensive, scandalous daughter who forced my way into her world despite the abortion-inducing herbal teas she drank and her frantic leaps off of small buildings.

When I am sixteen, my father calls me on the phone to, inevitably, weep. He says, "Living in this country, I have learned not to hope for things. Only you are my hope. Only you."

So—yes, I grow up fast.

we live up here

roxy has a secret and i know it.

roxy—fresh
from the dominican republic—
lives on the first floor
and me—a haitian-talking
american—i live
on the third. she's twelve
years old
and i'm nine but we're friends cuz
neither of us is allowed
to go outside. there is no play

for the daughters of immigrants
who rest under project ceilings.
we are our parents'
only investments.
in their dreams, we birth
second-story houses in the suburbs, strong
fences and theftless streets, jewish
neighbors walking well-groomed
dogs, graffitiless
two-car garage doors.

there is no room
in our parents' fantasies
for the brown
folks of our dreary daily lives
who work or loiter or love
or die around us. who don't know

coconuts and guava, mango
and quenepas. who don't muse over
lost motherlands and ancestral languages
the way we do.

here we are kept
away from the dark
men who grab
their nuts, blare
boombox blasphemy and deal
medicinals that never heal. i say,
there are great expectations
and no play
for the daughters
of immigrants.

so when roxy and i get in from school
or church, we poke protected
heads out of our respective,
scraped windows and witness
hood rat games of tag, ambulance
arrivals, d.s.s. departures, welfare
check elation, various evictions
and arrests. we watch our people
who are not our people
from the safety of our homes.

roxy's english is still
thick with spanish
and mine's so thoroughly bred
in cambridge, massachusetts, that we avoid
speaking to each other. instead we communicate

by lifting bored brows, frowning or rolling
our eyes. sometimes she asks me
what curse
words mean—slut, asshole, screw—
and when i tell her, sometimes she smiles.

but most times roxy hates me
cuz i am her
mirror: trapped and also brown.
i throw down
the drawings i make of her.
she winks
up at me, fellating
bananas
and in this way, we are
close.

roxy has a secret and i know it:
while her parents are asleep—or out
waging their undocumented minimum—
roxy has a white boy
climbing
in and out of her
first-floor window.
he's irish and athletic, in high
school and cute. he
brings beer.

roxy sticks her sepia
arms out—pulls
him through her plastic pane,
into her prison

which i imagine is painted pink and stinky
with perfume, cluttered
with neglected porcelain dolls, purple
diaries plastered with stickers of fake
locks and keys
that probably never get used.

for hours, i wait, missing
the top of roxy's head
as i imagine moans and firm
bananas going mushy
on her thighs, inside. eventually,
it is time for him to leave and i spy
his lean body withdrawing
from her bedroom, his tongue
fast-knocking the roof
of her mouth. she whispers,

te amo and he mutters
también like
tom-ben and she giggles
like the girls do
in the movies. and me and roxy
rest rapunzel-like
elbows on our sills—palms
crushing the faint chin hairs
we will later pluck to feel
more american. we become

women as we study
her boyfriend's flat butt, fleeing
our end

of this broken world, back
to his house in the 'burbs.

one day my mother says, i am so glad
we live up here. and that's how i guess
roxy's secret is out.
i hear noises
through her window
now: an aging mother hailing
mary loudly, a father
weeping then breaking
things, beating her.
and when she finally hangs her head

out of the window again, i say, hi,
over and over—then ask, where
is your boyfriend? to which she replies,
screw you, asshole! and i think,
slut—but dare not pitch it.

these days, roxy wears
the sweatshirts the missing
boyfriend gave her
to conceal the swell of her
belly. these days, roxy
wears headphones, repeating
the standard inflections she hears, trying
to sound like the new
american daughter
she's expecting in the fall.

gift a sea

after i became
grandfather called me dry
nasty names
stood small in my kitchen
baking hisses at midnight
praying rocks
against the women
in my love

but before
when i was tiny thirsty
he bought me a vintage typewriter
heavy and teal it splashed under my palms
a thrifted gift a sea in my blood
the first tool
my damp fingers used
to cool and name my self.

for how loudly

we will be remembered
for how loudly
the konpa comes from rubble
the dust of our fashion
and calves

we are the ones
conceiving in the mud
brushing teeth with hard kisses
braiding ribbon into lice
swilling tears for tea

never forget how the ghede
ground giddy
how we nicknamed our disaster
gentle taste:
gou dou gou dou

learn the hoarse voice song
of a tree of knowledge people
buck-naked good and evil
wild western mapou progeny
most deplored in the hemisphere
dissed and poor

and still here.

remember noah

you have to understand
it was so hot

sand as far as the eye could see
sand in teeth

a sealess life
every step a sinking a scratch

every storm
more sand

no sweat when we danced
pure salt in our lovemaking

i tried to spit once
it came out like a whistle

my first period
curry powder

old wives
spoke of tears

we thought they were
senile

laughter was
our wettest thing

we prayed often
to no one

we believed
in music

dry palms clapping
dust on ankle bracelets

we threw tabla and daff
caught spirit and sagat

a blaring life
the wailing of caesarean births

widows' eyes
wept wind

even our tongues were
tanned

something sun-dried
in every recipe

rays
were babies' first words

you have to understand
we forgot how to be thirsty

mud by then
was primitive

splashing
the stuff of legend

only giddiness
quenched us

we were dizzy all the time
in the world all the time

then we heard him
grumbling to himself

something about forty
something about a flood

clad in sheep's wool
he reeked of wolf shit

something about monogamy
something about shelter

i thought:
this must be heatstroke

i thought:
the brain of a six-hundred-year-old

i thought:
he is a conceptual artist

the ark
an installation

his masterpiece
took years

took trees
got bigger

he was our favorite
dirty joke

beloved schizophrenic
neighbor

then he started preaching
then he kidnapped pigs

mosquitos
doves

things that wanted to eat each other
stuffed onto the same boat

we threw our heads back
we slapped ashy knees

we mooned him
threw hot stones

we streaked
whistled in his face

kicked the baking
ship

laughter was
our thunder thing

the lucky ones died
laughing

for centuries
he warned us

condescending motherfucker
foaming at the mouth

sweat dripping
from his beard

condensation
how did we miss it?

i have no words for the first drop
cooling the cheek

grandfathers raised their arms
lightning made the children leap

sizzle gave way to drizzle
humidity taught humility

we opened our mouths
swallowing everything

the clouds begat clouds
began to bite us back

panic soaked
our slouching spines

the instruments
drowned first

we played them sopping
out of tune

denial gave way
to rivers

i fell into a puddle
my very first shiver

the shock of cold water
made me orgasm

so all the times before
had been dry heave?

so this was mourning
this was mikveh?

the sky from blue
to za'atar hail

we choked
god's vomit filled our lungs

apologies bellyflopped
reaching went out of reach

we ran from high desert
to highest mountain

to whirlpool
of choral grief

if noah had been merciful
he would have taught us how to swim

instead he saved
two mice

muttered prayers
shut the door

the best belly dancers
became mermaids

the dinosaurs learned
to fly

we never saw
a rainbow

our grave stones
coral reef

where our protest sound

jazz is underwater
vodou atlantis mute
aborted ultrasound
fetal fish in flood

haiti's first cousin
forcibly kissed
by a hurricane called
katrina. hot winds
come one fat
tuesday.
old levee leak
explodes. fixing funds gone
to homeland
security. soldiers
stationed in iraq. said,

jazz is underwater
days like laissez-faire
manna does not fall
saviors do not save

hunger prays to rage for
resilience. improvisational genius
implodes. anarchy duets
with despair.
bassist fingers loot—nimble
like a deft pianist. said, vodou
atlantis mute. the fragile
eardrums of instant orphans get

inundated with someone else's mama's
soprano saxophone screams.

(meanwhile televised tenor
voices report monotonous
drone to drown out)
the deafening beat
of funeral marchers
can't swim.
bloated trumpet
carcasses. a singer swallows human
sewage. her last note, a curse
on america. aborted
ultrasound. cacophonous

warnings scatter brains.
pedestrians hear calls to
evacuate, escape, and think, how
fast can on-foot run? the poor, the weary
just drown. abandoned elders
just drown. people
in wheelchairs just drown. the sick
in bed cannot leave. their doctors stay
behind too. new emergencies engulf
the e.r. swamped hospitals ain't
hostels, ain't shelters.

resources slim
like hope. nurses stay
behind too. their loyal partners
will not leave. ill-fated
rejects just drown. said, fetal fish

in flood. outside, a breaking
willow weeps like a father
on his rooftop, murmuring
his wife's last words: clutch tight
to our babies and let me
die, she had pleaded. you can't

hold on to us all, let me die.
she, too, like jazz, is
underwater. her love,
her certainty, will
haunt him. their children's
survival, a scar. sanity also
loses its grip. guilt-weight
like cold, wet clothes.
eighty percent of new orleans
submerged. debris lingers. disease
looms. said, days like laissez-faire.

manna does not fall. shock battles
suicide thoughts.
some thirsty throats cope,
manage dirges in cajun, in zydeco.
out-of-state kin can't
get through.
refugees (refugees?) remember
ruined homes.
a preacher remembers the book
of revelations. still saviors
wait to save.

and the living wade with the countless
dead while
a wealthy president flies
overhead
up where brown people look
up where
brown people look like
spoiled jambalaya, stewing
from a distance
in their down-there
distress. said,

he's free—
high up—far up—
vacation fresh—eagle up, up
and away
from the place
where our protest
sound started, still
sings. american music
gurgling cyclone litanies
man cannot prevent, the man
cannot hear.

quaking conversation

i want to talk about haiti.
how the earth had to break
the island's spine to wake
the world up to her screaming.

how this post-earthquake crisis
is not natural
or supernatural.
i want to talk about disasters.

how men make them
with embargoes, exploitation,
stigma, sabotage, scalding
debt and cold shoulders.

talk centuries
of political corruption
so commonplace
it's lukewarm, tap.

talk january 1, 1804
and how it shed life.
talk 1937
and how it bled death.

talk 1964. 1986. 1991. 2004. 2008.
how history is the word
that makes today
uneven, possible.

talk new orleans,
palestine, sri lanka,
the bronx and other points
of connection.

talk resilience and miracles.
how haitian elders sing in time
to their grumbling bellies
and stubborn hearts.

how after weeks under the rubble,
a baby is pulled out,
awake, dehydrated, adorable, telling
stories with old-soul eyes.

how many more are still
buried, breathing, praying and waiting?
intact despite the veil of fear and dust
coating their bruised faces?

i want to talk about our irreversible dead.
the artists, the activists, the spiritual leaders,
the family members, the friends, the merchants,
the outcasts, the cons.

all of them, my newest ancestors.
all of them, hovering now,
watching our collective response,
keeping score, making bets.

i want to talk about money.
how one man's recession might be

another man's unachievable reality.
how unfair that is.

how i see a haitian woman's face
every time i look down at a hot meal,
slip into my bed, take a sip of water,
show mercy to a mirror.

how if my parents had made different
decisions three decades ago,
it could have been my arm
sticking out of a mass grave.

i want to talk about gratitude.
i want to talk about compassion.
i want to talk about respect.
how even the desperate deserve it.

how haitians sometimes greet each other
with the two words "honor"
and "respect."
how we all should follow suit.

try every time you hear the word "victim,"
you think "honor."
try every time you hear the tag "john doe,"
you shout "respect!"

because my people have names.
because my people have nerve.
because my people are
your people in disguise.

i want to talk about haiti.
i always talk about haiti.
my mouth quaking with her love,
complexity, honor and respect.

come sit, come stand, come
cry with me. talk.
there's much to say.
walk. much more to do.

because john doe is not a haitian name

a rotting smell
where the school once stood
a hungry shrill
where the guava tree grew
last night before the earth
ate port-au-prince
a bleeding orphan was
somebody's baby

and that somebody
was pretty or plain
and that somebody
was saucy or shrinking
and that somebody
made love, made mistakes
and that somebody
ate mosquitoes, chewed cane

and léogâne
served the lwa, praised the lord
and jacmel
danced well, clapped instead
and carrefour
had a temper, had a gift
and that somebody atop
a mass grave

knew marie, dieudonne, tantee
knew yves-pierre, jean-jean, timarc
who will christen

those who named us
with intention?
a poet also
died
in the earthquake.

her remains

when you come to dig up
a daughter deemed corpse, when you see
the smashed arm peek out of her
humiliated house, try to know
the bloated skeleton was
a woman once famous
for honey strut, machete
nerve and catching fire laugh.
you did not get to her in time.
arrive eventually and know
her remains wear her
very best dress.
silky as prayers, this dress.
a dried blood red, pressed
and tearless before
the torrent of cement.
study the sun-blanched photos she kept
in a polished, crushed chest, bestowed
by a new yorker, her favorite aunt
deemed distant mourner.
hold the dusty gold
around her decomposing neck.
a courting gift from the lover
who hates to survive her.
that lover there, weeping circles
right beside you, will never pardon
this taking earth
for shaking.
you are too late but come to salvage
the shattered remnants of this altar

she took her time to clutter with bottles
of amber rum, perfume, florida water.
these things
sacred, spilled now,
evaporated. hints and relics
of her want and breath.

no person

burn beloved
neighbor's flesh
for rotting in sun

bullet stray
dog for gnawing
charred lifeless meat

leave last daughter's
arm behind to save
first son's leg

slingshot white
dove to wage war
on walking hunger

no person on earth
should have to make
these choices

forget
that you are
person

life is another word

a reporter will tell you
once
that a haitian woman was raped
then forced to perform sex acts
on her twelve-year-old son
by a masked gang of neighborhood
teenagers in west palm beach
florida in the dunbar village projects
only some of us knew
existed

the reporter is paid
to deliver this news
with a straight if solemn face
with the same grave
tone he uses to report a suburban
house on fire
another soldier down
a snow storm on its way
a car crash that results in a traffic jam
you really ought to dodge

as if severe facts can be edited
down to consumable
sound bites
as if sound bites are effective
warnings
as if learning the mere
who what when and where
can soften

the blow
of the how

as if the son will not vomit
when a future lover suggests
putting a mouth anywhere near him
as if his brain won't bleed
from trying to squeeze
flat
the memory of his mother's
trembling lips
approaching his aroused
shame

inching toward him
as if she were stumbling aboard
a slave ship oh the terror
of knowing that if she survives this
she is somehow expected to breathe
to keep breathing
to keep living
as if life
is not another word for
remember

oral sex on her twelve-year-old
son
as if a violated child
is anyone's child anymore
as if the definition of mother—
to nurture, to protect—
has not been evenly beheaded

you know beheadings are irreversible
once you have been cut off
you are cut off

even if you are chicken
even if your body still
feels
the sting of the slice
even if you manage to run
your inevitable last thought is
something has been
irrevocably severed
in the case of the assailants
it was their hearts

but maybe they were born without them?
poverty causes
birth defects undetectable
until a child becomes
a criminal oh america
your children
are cannibal gunmen
they murder people
who look like them
your children are diseased

their veins pump your war
blood your dormant gene
awake and rabid your
antecedent virus catching
your unspoken cancer history
screaming malignant your martyr's

mother's curse manifesting the globe
you set on fire is burning you
alive these american boys
are dead

long before they have grown
their first stubble
they are trouble
bubbling in the wake of rubble
of psychological warfare
come flesh
a poet will tell you
a thousand times
this shit is
not poetry:

ten rapists ages fourteen to eighteen
took turns
taking a woman
could have been their mother
rammed a train into her anus
pushed her into a bathtub full
of vinegar water hydrogen peroxide
alcohol ammonia nail polish
remover they beat her
held a gun to her head

made her give head
to the one she had given birth to
recorded their torture
with a cell phone camera
as if replaying it would keep it

more real
maybe they were replaying
an ancestral memory?
what happened africa
before the middle passage?

maybe they were playing
slave captor and slave
the way some kids play cowboys
and indians cops and robbers
soldier and abu ghraib prisoner
you know one of them
used a condom
had planned far ahead enough
to purchase or steal
one condom

as if the aids he worried the immigrant
woman might have was the worst thing
he could get
he could get life in prison
they will be tried
as the men they never got to be
were never fathered by
do not even know
america your headless
heartless young

do not even
know life
is another word for
remember

i tell you
they will never forget
their crimes
the way you
have forgotten
them.

mayday

what are we going to feel
when it's us?

when hive planes corrupt
a sky above ducked heads?

when water dirty,
when thirst?

when every utterance within earshot
italicized, exclaimed?

what
when the ceiling tarpaulin?

when sidewalk for hospital,
rubble for sidewalk?

when sticky faces
of neighbors statistic?

when all the home we knew
news now,

we will want someone to call it
war then—

to mark our rowdy graves
by name and not circumstance—

to imagine our eyes
beneath bull's-eyes—

to spare the children
expired medicine.

when will we realize
it is already us?

scrubbed and guilty—
it has always been us.

shopping, distant—
it will always be us.

bloodletting, forgetting—
can't stop that it's us.

every life on this planet
reflects mine.

every body torn into,
every soldier shorn,

every wall erected,
every murderer

mourned,
adorned.

every death, every breath
on this planet

expects mine,
implies us.

so what
have we realized?

and how
are we feeling?

for the sore

not every poem a gong
not every poem a trumpet pressed
to the calloused lips
of the wronged some

for sneaky street kisses
some for holy shameless tongue
can't always write
damage dirge dictum

this song for the sore
heart's soar
this murmur rise above
its roar

some anthems what
the corpse would sing
if he could
oh if she could

this verse for bare
heels on hard wood
for healing blush
of soaked palm

for wet wrinkle
of a slack middle
finger used to smooth
the mean from my brow

this hymn soft hum
for the autumnal sway
of unopened bills
that dry a bathroom floor

not every poem
gas and match some
hover wonder steam
this one

for a phoenix
to rest in midair
to clean smoking
feathers

can't every line burn
yes joy will take
its turn and i
forgive myself

self-portrait as a heel

your dreadlock crown
your square teeth of america
oh grimace of port-au-prince
oh tags on helmet
door
you found
you objet d'art
barefoot in bum-rushed studio
so bebop boxer brave
so basquiat
a canvas on corruption
an ancient eshu magic
you mocked van gogh for breakfast
skipped lunch to piss with warhol
kicked for screamers
kinged the sons of slaves
you black you fight
you gray played
clarinet you could not play
clear as cassius clay
disheveled crown
you punk rock auction block
mishap randy rap
art world spit
misfit
you prophet by design
free for fee
so radical
oh feeler

oh sensitive pensive ghoul
you uptight bass
upright animal
minimalism middle-fingered
namer of same old shit
oh million-dollar it boy
your flippant brush
your brush with death
you rode
his old white
bones
golden crown
majestic mona lisa scribble
smile
you charlie chaplin parker
park bench avenue
new wave
new dare
new devil
divine in details
you colored show
museum bust
you rust
you anxious bite
obnoxious liberals knocked
you let them in
exed them out
lived off exes
sucked their collars
como chicken
then heroin for dinner
then island eyes

then grief for sale
a war subliminal
a subway token
oh broken crown
oh high art fears
oh hunter's tears
oh cursing clown
lo urban game
colonial woe
cristobal colonoscopy exhibit
you fury of puerto rico
you fort
your art for soup
you set that on fire
paint-splattered armani suit
you exposed root
bleeding family tree
brilliant fallen leaf
you left us
high on glyphs
chest exhumed
you vehicular treasure
exhausted heart on walls
oh winged
oh worn
oh hiccupped warning
oh earthling trophy
knife woe life
trophonius
woe error
yo hero
so overdose

so clever man
a dozen in a zillion
you flag stuck in knees
you juice for joints of jumpers
we leap because you leapt
i weep
we never met

a pump of bony pelvis

cover your mirrors
a phantom has passed
in the end
we will all look
like michael jackson

a hypnotist
dandy
sexy spirit of corpses
vodou's ghede in sunglasses
a pump of bony pelvis

he he was as pale
as a manga superhero
as smooth as zorro
a limber zombie
singing thriller

a minstrel
in reverse
a gloved black power fist
curled tight around an aching
crotch (daggonnit baby ow)

oh michael i loved you
you king without borders
you emotional pauper you pop
you sure-footed lunatic
you flying lost peter

your irresistible girl voice
floating out of a grown man's
ever-shifting timeless
chiseled troubling face
you were your own race

you mess of delicious gender
you queer jolly roger
you masturbation good
you lover not a fighter
you earth-quaker

you perfect music maker
you screaming-fan-fainter
you fedora flicker
you james brown snicker
you slicker

he he was a childish child embracer
our american disaster
our american anthem
the original idol
gaudy godlike only man

ultimate
crossover
act
irrevocably crossed
over

his graceful genius
body

gone
too soon
too soon

said, cover your mirrors
to hear the ghede laughing
but in the end we are still
looking
for michael jackson

silence equals death

Family.
Family.

They pretended not to see, not to know you, why you disappeared so sudden. No more short and careful letters on expensive, lavender paper to appease them with currency and signed half-truths. No more tooth piercing tongue to crush your lisp while you muttered, "Everything is fine," into crunching phone receivers. No more giggles to mask your chagrin. "No, no, no. No marriage yet," you said.

You paid for long distance.
You paid.

"But it has been three months!" Four. Seven. They discussed among themselves, confirmed your silence toward them all and felt better or sincere when they whispered their concern. Did they love you? Did they miss you?

You were blood.
You were blood.

But they pretended not to know why when the news came of your collapse on the West Side Highway. A white man saw you, recognized emergency, sent for sirens. Then doctors with thick gloves examined your heart-shaped anus, torn. Your torn heart, shameful as shit. Your frail figure, fucked more frail with a then new, burning virus. You lost your mind. You blamed yourself.

You, blamed.
You blamed your blood.

Uncle, I want you to know: I was ten years old, I saw you.
When we visited, I saw the straight-porn glossies scattered
obvious at the foot of your queen-size bed. How they
contradicted the half-used douche in a bathroom cabinet
you never shared with a woman. I saw tight jeans—a pair
in every rainbow color—snug around your bones. You
were as stickly as a model, a well-known chef who never
ate.

I saw the man you were always with—who my mother kept
calling your best friend. How you watched him like the
clouds. How he barely touched you. How he kept a wallet,
thick with snapshots of two tiny, toothless children. And
his lovely, skinny wife. A blonde, bleached.

"Yeah, I've met her," you told us.
"She hates me," you said.

Then your best friend sort of winked and whisked you off
in his black jag to take you out, "For ice cream," he said.
But that stench on your breath when you returned from
the trip was not as pleasant to me as ice cream. And you
forgot to bring us some.

Uncle, I was only ten, but I want you to know I saw: The
tubes fisting your every orifice. The grayness of you,
flattened on your hospital bed. The unchosen silence. No
more breathing on your own. No more T cells in your

spirit. No more clues in the abandoned apartment your landlord had ransacked.

And not one friendly fuck from a bathhouse. Not one drunken buddy from a nightclub. Not one best friend with his family's fading photos or his wallet to sit beside you, to tell a simple story, to confess exploded truth.

Just a room full of doctors who—though they kept listing cancers—must have sworn more silence, weakly crafted to protect you from your family full of strangers who were hungry and feigned confusion as they sang hymns in French and prayed in Haitian-Kreyol to the Lord they believed might have seared folks like us.

Uncle, when I looked, I saw: Graceful Erzulie in your hips. Worry tacked onto your brow. The pink of your tongue. The stretch marks and slits at the corners of your glossy lips. The crisp King's Bible on your coffee table. The satin sheets on your wide, queen's bed. The burgundy stains on the asylum-white linens of your intensive care cot.

I saw the heart.
I saw the heart monitor's cruel, blue line.

How it accompanied a final, blaring
bleeeeeeeeeeeeeeeeeeeeeeeeeeeeeeeeep.

madivinez

mommi.
in the apartment i share
with the woman
i love, we have
a bright yellow bookcase, used
as an arts altar. we shelve
crayons, watercolors, ink, paper
and glue for collages. i keep
my haitian-kreyol-english dictionary
behind the colored pencils.

its red cover taunts me, daily.
i am often too afraid
to open it. i picked it up once—
when i first got it—hungry
for familiar
words that could make me
feel home. i tried
to look up lesbian
but the little red book denied
my existence.

i called you, remember?
mommi. how do you say
lesbian in kreyol?

oh, you said,
you say madivinez but
it's not
a positive word.

it's vulgar.
no one wants
to be
called madivinez.
it's like saying
dyke.

but how
can cruelty sound
so beautiful?
madivinez
sounds so glamorous.
something i want
to be. madivinez.
my divine?
sounds so
holy.

i thank you
and hang up the phone
to repeat
my vulgar
gift word
as i write it
into the dictionary,
next to ke,
kreyol
for heart.

glamorous, holy, haitian dyke heart.
something i want
to be.

malden, massachusetts

my mother won't feel
the knives inside her
tomorrow. a hysterectomy
requires general anesthesia.
we are severed from each other
these days. i work
in portland, art. she loses
sleep so watches cable
in malden, massachusetts.
she called to say she's proud
of me, my little brother's using
trojans, the doctors told her
fibroids and cysts fist
her uterine walls, hungry like
an unwanted child. it's all over with,
she mumbled in kreyol.
her birth-giving, she meant.
will you miss the blood?
i asked in english.
i miss you, she said.

seeing skinhead

Last summer, I had an encounter with a skinhead on the #1 train in New York City.

My partner and I were headed uptown—back to the little, lightless, roach-infiltrated Upper West Side studio we had creatively spun into a mildly cozy, albeit temporary, home. I was in the middle of two demanding and exhilarating months, making challenging off-Broadway theater. I was also having the worst period cycle of my entire existence, complete with the kind of violent, seizing megacramps that remind me that soldiers are exploding, children are starving, salmon is an endangered species, and the earth is burning and melting all at once. I should have been thrashing in bed all night, but I had no understudy. As they say, the show must go on.

On the humid night I met the skinhead, I had been on stage for hours playing a haunted, brooding, sexy, defiant rock star. My voice was hoarse from singing my guts out. My muscles ached from the fast-paced dance moves. Knowing that I was in a state that demanded tender escort, my partner picked me up after the show.

The train we boarded was packed and rancid. We sat across from a rangy white man with a grumpy disposition. He wore dirty, baggy camouflage pants, a military cap and unlaced combat boots. After a couple of uneventful stops, he began to softly pitch the word "waste" in my direction.

"You're a waste," he said over and over. It sounded like spit. "You're a waste."

My cramping uterus caught fire. Flames rose in me like pending volcanic vomit. I had visions of myself hurling fire through him like some sort of antiracist dragon. Bursting into mortal combat. Reaching past his chapped lips into his big mouth to yank out the hate, to squish his wicked, filthy tongue in my hands like a frenzied chef shaping ground beef.

Instead I took a deep breath. I channeled my outrage into a form of meditation. I reminded myself that I am a writer. My job is to observe and to remember. When push comes to shove, memory is my greatest self-defense. I can be a warrior but I would rather be a poet. Poets live longer.

I challenged myself to make direct eye contact with my loud-mouthed opponent. At first he seemed delighted by my gall. He raised his eyebrows, managed a smirk and dared to insult me louder. "You're a waste of the human genome," he shouted. The other train passengers froze.

I wasn't sure if his comment was about race, gender, or my apparent intimacy with another woman, but he was clearly picking a fight. He pulled off his cap to reveal and rub his bold, bald head. I scanned this wannabe monster for clues—proof of a broken inner child, a cracked mind, a shard of humanity. I told myself if I could find his humanity, I wouldn't have to kick his ass. He started chanting "waste" again. Like a baby who had learned a new word. Like it was the only word he knew.

Stops came and went. The car was mostly quiet. My partner asked me if I wanted to move, but I slowly shook my head no. By now, I was totally consumed. And as I assessed him, something in me unexpectedly softened. I noticed his poor posture, his fidgeting hands. The tiny— almost timid—swastika tattoo on his right inner wrist. His dirty, chewed and bleeding fingernails. His intimidated, wandering eyes.

When I finally registered his countless missing teeth, I thought, Surely this skinhead has verbally assaulted strangers before. Surely some of those strangers have instinctively pounced on him. Surely those strangers had cracked his bones and called him "cracker" and perhaps felt justified, righteous and brave in doing so. Surely they had taken it upon themselves to teach him a severe lesson. And maybe—as he fought or squirmed or pleaded or cursed beneath them—the skinhead secretly rejoiced in their rage because it was attention, after all. Maybe the skinhead felt most alive and strong and worthy and meaningful when he was fighting someone—anyone. Maybe he wasn't in it for the lesson, but for sucking energy. Maybe he was trying to use me to feel alive again.

I refused to be used. I simply didn't have the energy to spare.

I stared at him.

I stared at him and eventually his volume grew weaker. He seemed to realize that he could call me "waste" all he wanted and all he would get was a witness. A witness to the hunger, neediness, madness, cowardice, loneliness and fear he pretended was hate.

And do you know what happened next? The racist skinhead said, "Thank you." He thanked me! Then he looked away and stopped speaking altogether.

My partner and I got off at 96th Street. We emerged from the bowels of the Big Apple hand in hand—unscathed, if a bit shaken. Later she told me that she and the other train passengers had quietly stared him down too. We had been an army of witnesses.

We live to tell the tale.

elephant mourning

paste blank pages
into this blank journal
a sticky collage
of space and silence

press the glue here
to smother the screams except
too many children
are screaming

a trillion trumpets
i have elephant ears
i can sing but
there are no requiems

loud enough
to recall
to remember
replace

a blaring
a tearing
life
life

earth is paperback body
ripped in half
all the marks we have
made upon her gibberish

and i live
in a cheap crime novel
and she dies in baghdad
best seller

earth is crumpled
is paper is palestine
is child
is child's charred hand

bedtime stories blast
babar burns the poor
babies utter ivory
to sleep and sleep

can't amass enough
stubborn this mourning
to poet to speak
resurrection

in my spittle someone
else's blood spatters
in this pen all the ink
turned ashes

found few words here
where there are hot wars
in his mouth all the teeth
turned stones

found the grave site
the body's found poem

but the dead cannot read
these love letters

city library
of unshelved corpses
half-read books
like dried mouths ajar

could my words breathe
life back into
i would offer a trunk
full of plenty

letter to my father (in english)

this language i intend
to master this language i use
to sculpt a liberated life
to fight like haitian
for my art
for my wife

this is the language that stole
your time
your dreams
your daughter
so i speak lesbian
and you speak

unnatural
american
and we stop
speaking
to each other
father

love is my favorite word
i write it
with you in mind
as i live
with a woman
in my heart.

pray

pray for the people of haiti.
pray for ruined bellies, loose minds, rasping voices.
pray for cracked hearts that dance inside choleric bodies.
pray for the woman who cooks with amputated arm.
pray for the ground stood upon, slept upon, protested upon.
pray for the ground no longer trusted to stay still.
pray for the poets who salvage pens from uncleared rubble.
pray for the lwa to pardon the makeshift states of our altars.
pray for the man who sings his fist into lifting palm.
pray for the lovers whose fugitive moans rise above the
    unabated stench of death.
pray for the dead who shiver beside us.
pray for the children but first
teach them
to play.

desire

this restless night
this train track heart
these peeled eyes sore
this object red
this only thing
pedestal high
this will do the trick
this will
save my soul
this all i need
can make me whole
balled up fist
undulating palm
this giddy greedy
these gritting teeth
this tiger clutching
god's son's robe
this devil says uh huh
it could be yours
this instant
this urgent
the urge to leap
this hamster wheel rehearsal
of a memorized prayer
these rabbit-tap feet daring the captor
to steal another drum
this james brown beg
please please please
clitoral typing yes yes yes
this full-body nod

this jackson's ow
this black in heat
this cat in the gut
scratching at biting through
the butterfly yarn
this territorial bee
sting
this is mine
flight fused with fight
blood bound by hope
this now now now
this shoving the shoulders
of one's own fear
down down down
and out looking up
this heaven
this horizon
this faith
this moment fainted
oppressive tickle in the nostril
these smelling salts jolt
this stink of justice about to sneeze
this teakettle scream
this bitten bottom lip
this creole this gospel
this blues this be-bop
this reggae
this hurled rock
this sinner sound
comforts have-nots
this lime green saliva
this plain old thirst

running crazed
toward the fire hose
to beckon the bull
this l'ouverture gallop
this tubman pull
this guevara stomp
this straight-backed spat-on student
stays sitting in
this beat-box be the new drum
this b-girl be kali
this noose loosened to necklace
of round white skulls
this head spinning holy
this ghost caught looting
this katrina survivor riot
this possession we possess
this zombie life threatening
to live
to keep living
this vodou ache what make
revolution.

anahata

aside from faith,
as far as you know,
you will never have another heart.
better to grow the one you were born with.
fill it with blood and love. risk.
let the strange world sneak inside.
accept all of life in your chest.
death is the end of percussion.
breathe deeply, the music
will function. listen close.
freedom thaws in your ribcage.
dance with vehemence
to feel its fast-pumping.
tempt two lips to greet your throat
and take note: your racing pulse
will laugh and kiss back. god is strong
in the clock of your desire.
every tick, my friend, divine
confirmation: you are alive. beat. yes!
you are alive.

acknowledgments

Many of the poems in this collection are featured in the author's solo performances. A number of the pieces were previously published in *Platte Valley Review, Make/Shift, Utne Reader* and *Meridians,* as well as in the anthologies *Word Warriors: 35 Women Leaders in the Spoken Word Revolution, Does Your Mama Know: An Anthology of Black Lesbian Coming Out Stories,* and *Brassage: An Anthology of Poems by Haitian Women.*

Thanks to the theaters, colleges, festivals and venues that welcome these words. Thank you loved ones. Thank you Hedgebrook for your radical hospitality. Thank you Gaea Foundation for the Sea Change Residency. Thank you Astraea for awarding writers. Thank you Nancy Bereano for your red-pen brilliance. Thank you Martha Richards for your acts of encouragement. Thank you Vanessa Vargas for seeing this poet through.

about the author

Lenelle Moïse creates jazz-infused, hip-hop-bred, politicized texts about identity, memory and magic. She was a 2012–2014 Huntington Theatre Company Playwriting Fellow; her plays include *Merit*, *Expatriate*, *The Many Faces of Nia* and *Cornered in the Dark*. Moïse was the 2010-2012 Poet Laureate of Northampton, Massachusetts. *Haiti Glass* is her first book. www.lenellemoise.com

Printed in the USA
CPSIA information can be obtained
at www.ICGtesting.com
JSHW082003230524
63699JS00002B/50